First Bible Stories

For Francesca Dow

MM

For Fara

NS

First edition for the United States and Canada
published exclusively 1998 by Barron's Educational Series, Inc.
First published in Great Britain 1998
by Orchard Books
Text © Margaret Mayo 1998
Illustration © Nicola Smee 1998

Address all inquiries to:
Barron's Educational Series, Inc.
250 Wireless Boulevard, Hauppauge, NY 11788

Library of Congress Catalog Card No. 97-36433

International Standard Book Number 0-7641-5082-0

Library of Congress Cataloging-in-Publication Data
Mayo, Margaret.
   First Bible stories / retold by Margaret Mayo; illustrated by
Nicola Smee.
      p.   cm.
   Summary: Retells stories from the Old Testament, including stories
about Adam and Eve, Noah, Joseph, Moses, and Jonah.
   ISBN 0-7641-5082-0
   1. Bible stories, English—O.T. [1. Bible stories—O.T.]
I. Smee, Nicola, ill. II. Title.
BS551.2.M374   1998
220.9'505—dc21   97-36433
                                                                        CIP
                                                                        AC

Printed in Belgium
9 8 7 6 5 4 3 2 1

First Bible Stories

Retold by Margaret Mayo

Illustrated by Nicola Smee

BARRON'S

CONTENTS

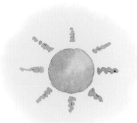

SEVEN SPECIAL DAYS

How the World Was Made

I n the beginning, it was always dark, and the earth was covered with deep water. There were no people, no animals, no birds, no fish, and no sun, moon, or stars.

But God was there, and He was the one who decided to make the world. And how did He begin?

He just said, "Light!" And there it was. Bright and wonderful light. Everywhere.

But God didn't want it to be light all the time. "After light, I'll have some dark," He said. "Then some light again. Turn about. I'll call the light time…DAY, and the dark time…NIGHT." And so God made the first day and first night.

"That's good," He said. He was pleased.

Then came Day Two. And what did God make next?

He said, "Sky!" And there it was. Blue sky, stretching over the water.

But God thought the sky looked empty. He said, "Clouds!" And there they were. Big puffy clouds and soft swirly clouds, floating across the sky.

"That's good," said God. He was pleased.

Day Three came. Now—what next?

God said, "Earth! Some here and here! There and there and over there!"

The deep water heaved and rolled, and land rose up and up, out of the water. Big rocky mountains, smooth flat places, humpy hills, and river valleys. Little islands and huge spreading lands.

But God thought the land needed some color. He said, "Green grass! Flowers, vegetables, bushes, trees! Grow! Spread and make new plants!" And there they were. Every plant you can think of. Roses and lilies, daisies and poppies. Trees hung with apples, oranges, and shiny cherries. Cabbages, strawberries, and beans.

"That's good," said God. He was pleased.

Then came Day Four. Now—what next?

God thought the living plants would need a time to be warm and a time to be cool, a time to grow and a time to rest.

He said, "Golden sun! You'll be in charge of the day and bring warmth to earth. Silver moon! You'll be in charge of the night. Silver stars! Join the moon and twinkle in the nighttime sky."

And there they were: the sun shining in the day, and the moon and stars at night.

"That's good," said God. He was pleased.

I'M PLEASED

Then came Day Five. Now—what next?

God thought the water and the air needed some life and color. First he said, "Swimming creatures, fill the water!" And there they were. Enormous whales, playful dolphins, and sharp-toothed sharks. Shellfish, jellyfish, silvery fish, spotted fish, and striped fish.

Then God said, "Flying creatures, fill the air!" And there they were. Butterflies, dragonflies, wasps, and bees. Sparrows and robins, noisy seagulls, cheeky magpies, bright-feathered parrots, long-necked swans, and high-flying eagles.

"That's good," said God. He was pleased.

Then came Day Six. So now—what next?

On Day Six, God looked at the land again, and He thought it still looked rather empty.

"It needs some moving-around life! Like in the water and the air!" He said. "So—moving creatures, fill the land!" And there they were. Elephants, lions, and tigers. Wolves and bears, cows and sheep. Cats and dogs. Snakes, lizards, and monkeys. All the living creatures that walk, crawl, run, jump, climb, and slither along…except for one kind.

"I haven't quite finished," said God. "I'm going to make one last thing. Something a bit like myself." He called out, "Man! Woman!" And there they were. The first handsome man and the first beautiful woman.

God said, "I'm going to put you in charge of all the living things I have made on the land, in the water, and in the air. I want you to take care of them."

The man and woman listened to God. "We will take care of everything!" they promised. "We will!"

"That's good," said God. He was pleased.

The next day was the seventh day.

"I have worked for six days," said God. "Now everything is finished. So, today, I'm going to rest."

And He did.

AND ON THE SEVENTH DAY I'LL REST

THE SNEAKY SNAKE AND
THE BEAUTIFUL GARDEN

The Story of Adam and Eve

Adam was the name of the very first man, and Eve was the name of the first woman. And at the beginning of time, when the world was fresh and new, they both lived, happy and content, in a garden God had made for them.

It was a beautiful garden. There were four rivers

winding through. It was full of lovely trees, flowers, and fruit, and all sorts of birds and animals. The sun shone each day, and it was never cold.

Now God told Adam and Eve that they could eat any of the fruit in the garden, *except for one kind.*

"Right in the middle of the garden stands a wonderful, beautiful tree," said God. "It is the Tree of Good and Evil. You must never eat its fruit. You mustn't even touch it. Or else…"

"Oh, we won't," promised Adam and Eve. "We won't!"

Adam and Eve often passed the Tree of Good and Evil. "It is a wonderful, beautiful tree," they thought. "And its fruit looks delicious." But Adam and Eve were careful not to touch any. They just looked.

One morning when Eve was standing beside the tree, just looking, a snake came along.

The snake was clever. The snake was cunning. The snake was sneaky. "*Mmmmmm*…that fruit is so-ooo delicious," the sneaky snake whispered softly. "Have you tasted it, Eve?"

"No," said Eve. "God said we must not eat it."

"Ah...now I'll tell you something," the sneaky snake whispered softly. "This is the Know-Everything Tree. If you eat its fruit, you'll be as clever as God." Then he whispered very softly, "Pick one, Eve. Pick one."

"I mustn't," said Eve.

The sneaky snake whispered very, very softly, "God won't see."

Eve peeped over one shoulder. She peeped over the other. Then she reached out her hand and picked a fruit.

Take one, Eve ....

16

"*Mmmmmm*…it is so-ooo delicious," the sneaky snake whispered very, very softly.

Eve opened her mouth, and she bit into the fruit. "*Mmmmmm*…it *is* delicious!" she said. "I must give some to Adam!" And off she ran.

As soon as she found him, she whispered softly, "Adam…taste this."

"But," said Adam, "that's a fruit from the Tree of Good and Evil. We mustn't eat that fruit! We mustn't even touch it!"

"*Mmmmmm*…it is so-ooo delicious," Eve whispered very, very softly. "Taste it, Adam…taste it. God won't see." And she gave the fruit to Adam.

He opened his mouth and bit into the fruit. "*Mmmmmm*…it *is* delicious!" he said.

And then—they finished the fruit between them.

Most evenings, God came and walked in the beautiful garden and talked with Adam and Eve. It was always a happy time.

But that evening, when Adam and Eve heard God walking in the garden and calling their names, they were frightened.

"I don't want God to see us," said Adam.

"Let's hide," said Eve.

They found some large leaves and wove them together, and they each made a sort of skirt. They dressed themselves in the skirts. Then they hid among the trees.

ADAM! EVE!

WHY DID YOU DO THIS ?

But God found them.

"Why have you covered your bodies with leaves?" He asked. "And why were you hiding?"

Adam and Eve looked at the ground, and they closed their mouths tight shut.

God said, "Have you picked the fruit from the Tree of Good and Evil? Have you tasted the fruit I told you not to eat?"

Adam and Eve still looked at the ground, and they still kept their mouths tight shut.

"Why did you do this?" asked God.

"It wasn't my fault," said Adam. "Eve picked the fruit. She told me to eat it."

"Eve," said God. "Why did you do this?"

"It wasn't my fault," said Eve. "It was the sneaky snake. He told me to pick the fruit. He told me to eat it."

God was sad. "Adam and Eve," He said, "because you have disobeyed me and eaten the fruit from the Tree of Good and Evil, you will have to leave the beautiful garden forever."

Now Adam and Eve were sad and sorry. "What will happen to us?" they asked.

"From now on," said God, "you, and your children after you, will have to work. You will dig the hard ground. You will pull up thorny bushes and prickly thistles. And the sun will not always shine for you."

But God still cared for Adam and Eve, and He showed them how to make clothes from animal skins, so that they would not be cold when they left the beautiful sunny garden.

"I will not forget you," said God. "I will always love you. You are the people I have made."

Then He led Adam and Eve out of the beautiful garden. And they never ever came back.

NOAH AND
THE VERY BIG BOAT

The Story of the Flood

Long, long ago, there was a good, kind man called Noah. He lived on a farm with his wife, his three grown-up sons, and his sons' wives. They were a happy family who loved God and the beautiful world God had made.

But the rest of the people had become very wicked.

They hated each other and were always stealing, fighting, and killing.

They made God so sad He decided to start the world over again. He said, "I'll ask that good, kind man called Noah to help me."

One hot, sunshiny day Noah was just strolling around his farm, when God said to him, "Noah, I want you to build a very big boat."

Noah wrinkled his nose and frowned. "I don't need a very big boat," he said. "There isn't any sea around here."

"That's true," said God. "But I'm going to send lots of rain and make a flood. So I want you to build a boat big enough to hold you and your family…two of every animal…two of everything that flies…two of every creepy-crawly creature…and enough food to last for a long time."

"It will have to be a VERY BIG boat," said Noah.

"It will indeed," said God. And then He told Noah exactly how to build the very big boat.

NOAH, I WANT YOU TO BUILD A VERY BIG BOAT

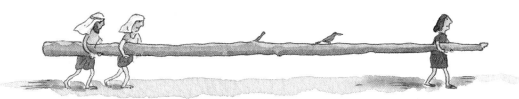

Next day, Noah and his family began to build the boat. It was hard work. They chopped down trees. They cut them into planks, shaped and smoothed the planks, and fitted them together.

The wicked people watched. And how they laughed. "What's that? A BOAT!" they shouted. "Silly old Noah! Who needs a boat on dry land?"

"There's going to be a flood," said Noah. And then they laughed some more.

Silly old Noah! Ha Ha

At last the boat was finished. But then—more hard work. Noah and his family began to collect armfuls of hay…sacks of corn…bags of nuts…baskets of fruit and vegetables…all the food they could find. They carried it onto the boat and filled every storeroom, cupboard, and shelf, every nook and cranny.

As soon as everything was packed, something amazing happened. Just imagine. From every side animals came running, birds and insects came flying, and lots of strange creatures came creeping and crawling. Two by two they came, moving together like friends. God had sent them.

"Come in," called Noah. "Come right inside."

And they all went into the very big boat, and Noah and his family found a place for each one to lie down, sit or stand, curl up or perch.

Then Noah closed the big door of the very big boat. CLUNK!

He looked out of the window and waited. Nothing happened. For seven days and seven nights, Noah waited. Had God forgotten about the flood? No, He hadn't. At long last rain came splitter-splattering down.

It rained, and it rained, *and it rained*. For forty days
and forty nights, it rained. And a swooshing, swirling
flood of water rose up UP UP. It covered every house,
every tree, the hills, even the highest mountains.

Everything that lived and moved on land was
drowned. But Noah's boat floated on the water, and
everyone inside the boat was safe.

All this time, what were Noah and his family doing? More hard work. They hardly had a moment to sit down and rest. There were so many hungry mouths and wide-open beaks to feed. And such a lot of cleaning.

Of course those animals, flying creatures, and creepy-crawly creatures were squashed up close together in the boat. There wasn't much they could do, except eat and sleep... and make a lot of noise. They were very good at that!

When at long last the rain stopped, God sent a powerful wind to dry up the water. WHOO–OOOO! it blew and blew. The flood went DOWN DOWN down…until one day there was a loud *scrunch!* The boat had come to rest on the side of a mountain.

Noah looked out the window. "I can see dry land!" he said.

His family cheered. "Let's open the door!" they shouted. "And go outside!"

"Not yet," said Noah. "We must find out if there's dry land everywhere."

Very gently, he picked up a dove, opened the window, and set her free.

The dove flew away and away. But she didn't find anywhere to land, and she soon flew back.

Noah waited seven days. Again he picked up the dove and set her free.

The dove flew away and away. Again she flew back. But this time she carried in her beak a fresh green olive leaf. So now Noah knew the water was lower than the trees.

He waited seven more days, and again he set the dove free. But this time she didn't come back.

Then Noah opened the big door of the very big boat and looked out at the fresh green sunshiny world. "Thank you, God, for keeping us safe," he said.

"Look up, Noah," said God. "Look up in the sky."

Noah looked, and he saw a glorious band of colors circling the sky. It was the first rainbow.

And God said, "I promise never to send a flood like this again. So, Noah, whenever you see the rainbow, remember my promise."

"Thank you," said Noah. "I will remember."

Then Noah called out, "My friends, it's time to leave the boat!" He didn't need to tell them twice.

Two by two, out they came—running, jumping, skipping, flying, creeping, crawling, slithering, or just plod-plodding along. And what a loud, happy noise they made! They were so glad to be outside and free.

Last of all, out came Noah's family. Then they and the animals, and the birds and flying insects, and the creepy-crawly creatures went off, this way and that, to build new homes and start new families in the fresh green sunshiny world.

THE SPLENDID, ABSOLUTELY MAGNIFICENT, RAINBOW-COLORED COAT

Joseph and His Jealous Brothers

J oseph was a happy boy who lived long ago in the faraway land of Canaan. His father Jacob was a rich farmer who had so many animals that it would have been hard to count them in one day.

Joseph had lots of brothers. *Eleven* altogether! Ten were older than he. But one—his name was

Benjamin—was younger. Joseph was especially fond of him, and, because their mother had died, he made a fuss of his little brother and gave him extra hugs.

Now of all his twelve sons, Jacob loved Joseph best. Benjamin was special too. But Joseph was his favorite, and, on his seventeenth birthday, Jacob gave him a wonderful present. It was a splendid, absolutely magnificent coat, bright and beautiful as a rainbow. There were stripes and patches of red, purple, blue, gold, green. In that coat, Joseph looked like a prince!

His older brothers were so cross and jealous. "It's not fair!" they grumbled. "Father never gave us a coat like that. Joseph is his favorite." And every time they saw Joseph wearing the coat, they became crosser *and crosser.*

One morning Joseph said to his
brothers, "Listen to this! Last night
I had two strange dreams. First we
were in the fields, tying up bundles
of corn, and my bundle rose up, stiff
and straight, and your bundles flopped
over and bowed to mine. Then I dreamt I was a star
and that the sun, the moon, and eleven stars bowed
down to me."

The older brothers were so very
cross. "We'll *never* bow to you!"
shouted Reuben, the eldest.

"*Never! never! never!*" they
all joined in.

A few weeks later, when the older
brothers were miles away, looking after
the sheep and goats, Jacob asked Joseph
to go and see his brothers and
bring back any news.

Joseph put on his splendid,
absolutely magnificent, rainbow-
colored coat, and off he strode.

When the older brothers saw him coming, all their angry feelings came bubbling up.

"Here comes the favorite," said one. "Let's kill him."

"No! Let's throw him into an empty well," said Reuben, the eldest. "And leave him there."

Then those rough, tough brothers grabbed Joseph, pulled off his coat, and dropped him into a deep empty well.

Poor Joseph. He couldn't climb out. He shouted and shouted. But his brothers took no notice.

Not long after, some
merchants came riding by,
their camels loaded with
perfumes and spices they
were taking to Egypt.

"Let's sell Joseph and make
some money!" said one of
the brothers. "We won't see
him again if he goes to
Egypt."

And that's what they did.
They lowered a rope and
pulled Joseph out of the
well. Then they sold him to
the merchants for just *twenty
silver coins*.

As soon as Joseph and the merchants were out of sight, the brothers began to wonder what to say to their father. They knew he would be very upset when Joseph didn't come home.

And those ten rough, tough brothers decided to tell a BIG LIE.

They ripped up Joseph's splendid, absolutely magnificent, rainbow-colored coat. They dipped it in some goat's blood. Then they took the coat back to their father.

"Look what we found on the road," they said.

"This is Joseph's coat," said Jacob. "He must be dead…A lion…or a bear…must have killed him…" And tears filled Jacob's eyes and rolled down his cheeks.

And poor Joseph—what about him?

He, too, had tears in his eyes, as he walked behind the swaying camels. He knew that when he got to Egypt the merchants would sell him to a rich man, who would make him work hard and wouldn't pay him any money.

"I'll be a slave in Egypt all my life," thought Joseph. "And I won't see my father or my little brother Benjamin ever again."

But things didn't work out quite like that. God had a plan for Joseph. His adventures had only just begun…

MORE STRANGE DREAMS

Joseph's Adventures in Egypt

When poor Joseph arrived at last in Egypt, the merchants sold him as a slave to a rich man called Potiphar.

Joseph worked very hard, and, because he was clever and good, Potiphar soon put him in charge of his house and his other slaves. And that would have been

the end of the story…

But—one day Joseph upset Potiphar's wife. He hadn't done anything wrong, but she was a nasty woman and made up mean lies about him. So poor Joseph was thrown into prison.

It was a sad time for Joseph. He didn't have any good dreams in prison, but when the other prisoners had dreams, they told them to him. He always knew what the dreams meant. *And those dreams came true.* Now that would have been the end of the story…

But—one night the king of Egypt had two very strange dreams, and he couldn't stop thinking about them. His wise men didn't know what the dreams meant. No one seemed to know.

One of the king's servants, however, had been in prison with Joseph, and one day, as he was pouring wine into the king's goblet, the servant whispered, "Your majesty, I know a clever man who understands dreams."

"Send for him!" said the king. "Right away!"

The captain of the prison was surprised when he was told the king wanted to see Joseph.

"Better shave off your bushy beard!" said the captain. "And put on some new clothes!"

So—*big rush and hurry*—and Joseph was ready. *More rush and hurry*—and he was at the palace, bowing to the king.

"I have heard that you're a wise, clever man who understands dreams," said the king. "So listen to my first dream. I saw seven big fat cows eating grass by the river. Along came seven thin bony cows, and—*gobble! gobble!*—they ate up the fat ones. But the thin cows didn't get any fatter.

"In my second dream, there were seven big fat grains of corn growing on a thick stalk. Beside them were seven tiny, dried-up grains growing on a spindly stalk, and—*gobble! gobble!*—the tiny grains ate up the fat ones. But they didn't get any fatter."

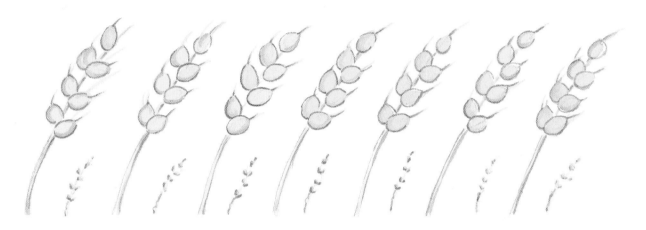

Joseph thought for a while. "Your majesty," he said, "the dreams mean there will be seven years of rich harvests with plenty of food. Afterwards there will be seven years when everything dies, and your people will be hungry."

"What shall I do?" asked the king.

"In the years of plenty, store all the leftover corn," said Joseph. "Then there'll be enough food when the hungry time comes. And, your majesty, I'd choose the wisest, cleverest man in Egypt to take charge of this."

"Joseph! *You* are the wisest, cleverest man I know!" said the king. And he took off one of his rings and slipped it onto Joseph's finger. He took his gold chain and hung it around Joseph's neck. "You shall be governor of all Egypt and second only to me!"

Suddenly—what a change for Joseph! The king gave him a large house and a splendid chariot. Joseph wore fine Egyptian clothes, and he soon married a lovely Egyptian girl. And before long he had two lively sons of his own.

The king's dreams did come true. For seven years there was plenty of corn in Egypt. Storehouses were built, and Joseph made sure that all leftover corn was heaped up, safe and dry, inside.

Then came the hungry times. There was no rain and the hot sun beat down. The grass and corn died, and there was not enough to eat.

So Joseph opened the store-houses, and hungry people came from near and far to buy corn.

Now far away in Canaan, Jacob and his family were hungry. But one day Jacob heard there was corn in Egypt, so he told his sons to go and buy some.

He wasn't happy about sending Benjamin. "Look after him," said Jacob. "He's my youngest son. Don't let anything happen to him."

"Don't worry! We won't come back without him," promised Reuben, the eldest brother. Then the eleven brothers rode off on their donkeys.

On the very day when the brothers came at last to the biggest storehouse in Egypt—*guess who was inside!* Joseph, the governor of all Egypt.

Joseph knew his brothers as soon as he saw them. He counted them. *Eleven altogether.* There were the ten rough, tough older brothers *and* the younger brother he was especially fond of—Benjamin.

But they didn't know Joseph, and when this grand man came up to them, *guess what they did!* They all bowed very low. Joseph's dream had come true!

Now Joseph wanted to know if his rough, tough older brothers were still cruel and unkind. Or had they changed? He decided to test them and find out.

So he pretended he couldn't speak the brothers' Hebrew language, and he said in Egyptian, "Who are you? Robbers? Thieves? Come to spy out where we keep our corn, so you can steal it?" Then a servant changed his words into Hebrew.

"No! No! We are honest men!" said Reuben, the eldest. "We are brothers. We have come from Canaan to buy corn."

"And your father," said Joseph. "Is he still alive?"

"Our father, Jacob, is an old man," said Reuben. "But he is alive and well."

When Joseph thought of his father, tears filled his eyes, and he had to hurry off so his brothers wouldn't see. But he hadn't finished testing his rough, tough older brothers. Not yet.

He said to his chief servant, "Tell those men to come
and have dinner at my house today."

The brothers were surprised when they were told
they had to go to the governor of Egypt's house. And
they were even more surprised when they entered that
grand house. They had never been in such splendid
rooms before, or seen so many beautiful dishes or such
splendid silver drinking goblets. Their father was rich,
but they had always lived in simple tents.

"Come," said Joseph quietly, in Egyptian, and he
pointed to where each brother had to sit. And he
placed them at a table in order of age. Reuben, the
eldest, first, down to Benjamin, the youngest.

"How does he know about us?" they murmured
to each other.

Joseph sat down at a separate table. He raised his very own splendid silver goblet so everyone could see it. The servants poured wine, and the feast began. You can imagine how happy those hungry brothers were when each was brought a plate piled high with all sorts of delicious food. But when they saw Benjamin's plate, they were so surprised, their eyes almost popped out of their heads! Benjamin's plate was HUGE, and there was FIVE TIMES more food on it than on the other plates.

"You're the favorite, Benjamin!" they joked. "Guess that governor must be especially fond of you!"

Joseph watched and listened. "My rough, tough brothers don't seem to be jealous of Benjamin," he thought. "Maybe they've changed."

But he hadn't finished testing them. Not yet.

Those hungry brothers enjoyed the feast. It was their first big meal for a long time. And they enjoyed talking to the governor of Egypt, who asked them lots of questions about their father and their families.

When the feast ended, Joseph told the brothers to go back to the storehouse and have their sacks filled with corn. So off they went, smiling and happy.

But then—*guess what Joseph did!* He picked up his own splendid silver goblet and gave it to his chief servant.

"Follow those men," said Joseph. "And when their sacks are filled with corn, hide my goblet in the sack of the youngest one, Benjamin. Afterwards, this is what you must do…" And Joseph whispered a secret in his ear.

Well, the brothers bought corn, loaded the sacks on their donkeys, and set off on the long journey home.

But they had not gone far when they heard the *drrrum! drrrum!* of horses' hooves. Joseph's chief servant was riding after them.

"Thieves! Robbers!" he yelled. "Stop!"

"We haven't stolen anything," said Reuben. "Look in our sacks and you'll see."

The chief servant opened one sack, then another and another. The last sack he opened was Benjamin's. And there— lying on top of the corn—was the governor of Egypt's very own splendid silver goblet.

Ohhh…the brothers were scared.

"We didn't take the goblet," said Reuben. "We are honest men. We didn't touch it."

"You must return to the governor's house immediately!" said the chief servant. So around they turned and back they went.

Ohhh…the brothers were even more scared. And when they were brought before Joseph, they bowed very, very low.

"We did not take your silver goblet," said Reuben. "We did not touch it."

Joseph glared at them. "The man in whose sack the goblet was found must stay in Egypt as a slave," he said. "The rest of you can go home."

"Please, please, let me stay instead," said Reuben.

"Our father loves Benjamin so much," said another brother. "He will die of sadness if Benjamin doesn't come home."

"Choose any of us," said another brother, "but not Benjamin."

Then Joseph knew that his rough, tough older brothers were no longer cruel and unkind.

He said to the Egyptian servants, "Go now! Leave the room." And when, at last, he was alone with his brothers, he said in his own Hebrew language, "I am Joseph."

The older brothers looked at him closely. Yes, he was Joseph, the brother they had sold as a slave. They trembled. Ohhh…they were more scared than ever.

"Don't be frightened. I'm not angry," said Joseph. "God looked after me. And perhaps I was sent here so that Jacob and his family wouldn't starve and die in this hungry time."

Joseph smiled. "Hurry home," he said. "Tell our father the good news. His son Joseph is alive! And he is governor of Egypt! Then tell him to come here and bring all the family, with their tents, servants, animals—everything. This is important, because the hungry time will go on for a few more years."

Then Joseph hugged Benjamin, the brother he was especially fond of. And then Joseph hugged his other brothers in turn. And after that his eleven brothers rode off home, with their sacks of corn and lots of beautiful presents from Joseph as well.

Jacob was so happy when he heard that his favorite son, Joseph, was still alive. Then it was—*big rush and hurry*—and they all packed their belongings. *More rush and hurry*—and the whole family, their servants, and their animals set off on the long journey to Egypt.

Of course when Jacob and Joseph finally met again, there were more hugs! And after that there was a great feast and lots of celebrations.

THE SECRET BABY IN THE BASKET

Clever Miriam, Moses, and the Princess

This is a story about a beautiful baby and a big sister who loved to sing and dance and shake a tambourine to make happy jingle-jangle music. Big sister's name was Miriam. *And* there's a princess in the story, too.

A long time after Joseph and his brothers died, their

great, very great-grandchildren still lived in
Egypt. There were lots of them, and they were
called Hebrews.

But there was a new king in Egypt who didn't like
them, and he decided to make them his slaves. Just like
that!

So the men had to work for him every day in the
hot sun. They dug out clay. They made bricks. They
built great huge treasure houses. *But* they weren't paid
any money, *and* they didn't have proper food to eat.

Then the king had another wicked idea. He ordered
that every Hebrew baby boy was to be thrown into the
river and drowned. Wasn't that cruel?

Now Miriam was a little Hebrew girl. She lived
with her mother and her brother Aaron. She
didn't see her father very often, because
he was a slave. That was sad.

At this time Miriam's mother was going to have a baby. Miriam kept hoping it would be a little girl. "But if it *is* a boy," she said, "I won't let anyone hurt him! I won't!"

Well, the baby was born—and it was a beautiful, cuddlesome baby boy.

"We must hide him," said Miriam's mother. "Here, in the house." And that's what they did.

Miriam and Aaron kept a lookout, and, if anyone came to their house, the baby was quickly hidden in a cupboard or a chest. When he cried, they took turns to hold him, rock him, and pat him.

But sometimes the baby opened his mouth and squalled—*Waaaaa…waaaaa!* Then Miriam snatched up her tambourine. And—*shakety-shake!*—she made jingle-jangle music, so that anyone outside wouldn't hear him. At the same time she sang and danced, to try and make her baby brother happy again.

When the baby was three months old, Miriam's
mother said, "We can't hide him any longer.
He's getting too big and noisy. But I have a plan…"

Miriam's mother took a basket and painted thick
sticky tar over the bottom, to make it watertight.
When it was finished, she laid the baby in this little
basket-cradle, and she kissed him. Then Aaron
and Miriam leaned over and kissed him.

Miriam and her mother carried the basket-cradle,
with the baby in it, down to the river and hid it
among tall reeds by the river's edge. This was a
special place, where a princess—one

of the king's own daughters—came to bathe
every day.

Then Miriam hid behind some bushes. But her
mother walked home.

After a while the princess came down to the river
with her servants. And the first thing she saw was
the basket. She looked inside.

"Ohhh!" she called out. "What a beautiful baby!"
That woke him, and he began to cry. "I didn't mean
to frighten you," she said, picking him up and
cuddling him. "But whatever are you doing here,
in a basket, by the edge of the river?"

"He must be one of the Hebrew babies," said one of the servants. "Well," said the princess, "I won't let anyone hurt him. I don't care what my father, the king, says. I'm going to keep him. He's going to be my little boy."

The next moment Miriam stepped out from behind the bushes. "Royal Princess," she said, "would you like me to find someone to look after the baby?"

"Yes," said the princess. "I shall need a nurse."

Miriam ran off. And when she came back, who did she bring? Her mother, of course!

"Feed this baby and take care of him till he is old enough to walk and talk," said the princess. "I'll pay you to do this."

"I shall be happy to look after him," said Miriam's mother as she stretched out her arms and took hold of her very own baby.

"And," said the princess, "I want his name to be Moses."

Now the baby was safe, *and* he had his mother, Miriam and Aaron to look after him and love him.

When Moses was older, he went to live at the palace and the princess brought him up as if he were her son. But he never forgot his own family, or his own people, the Hebrews.

Years later Moses became a powerful leader, and he helped his people run away from Egypt and go back to the land where Joseph and Jacob had once lived.

At the end of that great day, when they finally escaped, you can guess what Miriam did. She picked up her tambourine. And—*shakety-shake!*—she made happy jingle-jangle music and sang and danced and thanked God for looking after them. Before long, all the women joined in, shaking their tambourines, singing, and dancing. They were so glad to be free.

LITTLE BROTHER DAVID AND THE GREAT, HUGE GIANT

The Story of David and Goliath

Once there was a boy called David who had seven big brothers, and they were always bossing him around and telling him what to do. Big brothers can be like that. Sometimes.

David's father was a farmer, and he had lots of sheep that he kept in the hills outside the town of Bethlehem.

Baaa.

And David loved the sheep and their tiny lambs.

Right from when he was a little boy, he helped his big brothers look after them. He was very clever at finding any that got lost up in the high rocky places. And he wasn't afraid of all the wild animals prowling about those hills, looking for something tasty to eat.

David had a shepherd's staff. So if he saw a sharp-toothed wolf come slinketty-slinking toward the flock, he waved the staff and yelled "Yahoo!" and chased it away.

He also had a shepherd's sling. So if he saw a fierce lion or a big bear sneak-sneaking around, David put a stone into the sling. He whirled the sling around and around. Faster and faster! He let go of one end and the stone flew through the air. David was such a good shot! He hit the wild animals every time and frightened them away.

After a few years, David's brothers left him to look after the sheep all by himself. Even then he wasn't afraid. He had the staff and the sling. Besides, he believed that God, who made everything, was always with him and would look after him.

Then something happened that changed everything. Soldiers from the next country who were called Philistines came marching into Israel, the country where David lived. So David's three eldest brothers decided to go and fight in the king's army.

About five or six weeks later, David's father asked him to go and visit his soldier brothers and take them some fresh food from home.

David was excited. What an adventure! Now he would see the king's splendid army. He might even see the famous King Saul.

David asked a friend to look after the sheep while he was away. Then early next morning he set off, carrying a bag full of fresh-baked loaves and homemade cheese for his brothers. But he also took a shepherd's staff and a sling, just in case he met wild animals on the way.

David walked and he walked, and around midday he came to a valley between two high hills and…there were the two armies! The Philistine army was on top of one hill, and the army of Israel was on top of the other. But the soldiers weren't fighting. They were just standing there, glaring at each other.

When his brothers saw David, they were very cross. The eldest, whose name was Eliab, shouted, "David! What are you doing here? Who's looking after the sheep? Have you run away from home?"

David took a deep breath. "Father sent me," he said, "with some fresh-baked loaves and homemade cheese. They're for you."

He had just finished speaking, when suddenly—what a rackety noise! On the other side of the valley, the Philistines were shouting "*Hurrah! hurrah!*" and banging their shields—*clang! clang!*

Then everyone was quiet. They were waiting. What for? David looked about. And then the biggest, hugest, MOST GIGANTIC man he had ever seen strode forward and stood in front of the Philistine army. The man was a GIANT. From his feet, up to the top of his helmet, he was *nine feet tall!*

"I am Goliath, Champion of the Philistines!" he roared. "But where is your champion? You miserable cowards! Have you no one brave enough to fight me?"

The big brothers shuffled their feet and looked the other way. But David kept his eyes fixed on the giant.

"What was that about?" asked David.

Then his brothers told him that for forty days the two armies had been camped at the top of the two hills. Neither side was willing to move down and start the battle. But twice every day Goliath roared out his challenge.

"If we had a champion who could fight the giant and kill him, we would be the winners," said Eliab. "But if Goliath killed our champion, we would all become servants of the Philistines. But no one will fight a great, huge, GIGANTIC man like that!"

"I'll fight him!" said David.

Then his big brothers were crosser than ever. "You're so cheeky!" said Eliab. "You're only a boy. And that man's a giant and a trained soldier."

"I've fought lots of wild animals," said David. "I'm not afraid of him!"

The other soldiers smiled when they heard David arguing with his big brothers, and before long everyone was talking about the cheeky young boy. In the end King Saul heard that *someone was willing to fight the giant!*

"Bring him to me!" ordered the king.

But when David walked into the royal tent, the king was very upset. "You're only a boy!" he said.

"I know," said David. "But I'm not afraid of the giant. I've fought lions, wolves, and bears. God has always looked after me."

"Hmmm…there's no one else…well, all right," said King Saul. "But you'll need armor and weapons. Borrow mine."

Then David put on the king's armor. He looked very grand, but...

"This stuff is too big for me!" said David. He lifted a foot and tried to walk. "And too heavy! It *won't* do!"

So David took off the armor. He picked up his shepherd's staff and walked over to a little stream that was tumbling down the hill. He picked up five smooth round stones and put them in the bag where he kept his sling.

"Now I'm ready," he said.

The next moment there was that rackety noise again. The Philistines were shouting "*Hurrah! hurrah!*" and banging their shields—*clang! clang!*

Then everyone was quiet, and Goliath strode forward. "Miserable cowards!" he roared. "Where's your champion? Haven't you got *anyone* brave enough to fight me?"

David walked down the hillside. He jumped over the stream at the bottom of the valley. He looked up at the great, huge, GIGANTIC man.

"I'm not afraid of him," thought David. "God will help me!"

"Little boy, are you their champion?" Goliath roared. "And what's that stick for, *little boy?* Are you going to hit me with it?"

"Goliath," David called back, "you're a whole lot bigger than I. And you've got a sword and a spear. But I'm not afraid. My God will help me."

The giant was furious. "*Grrr…aaaaargh!*" he roared. And he came pounding down the hill with his spear pointing straight at David.

Quickly David put his shepherd's staff down on the ground. He took his sling and one smooth round stone out of his bag. He put the stone into the sling.

The giant came closer, closer, closer. David whirled the sling around and around. Faster, faster, faster. The stone flew out and it hit the giant—*wham!*—in the middle of his forehead.

Great, huge, GIGANTIC Goliath slowly toppled forward, and fell face down on the ground. He was dead.

Then—*what a rackety noise!* Now King Saul and his army were shouting "*Hurrah! hurrah!*" and banging their shields—*clang! clang!* They were so proud of David, their champion.

But when the Philistine army saw that Goliath was dead, they ran off as fast as they could. And King Saul's army chased them right out of the country.

After David killed the giant Goliath, his life changed. His big brothers didn't dare boss him around anymore, and he didn't go home and look after his father's sheep. Instead, he became a captain in the army, and, when King Saul died, David, who had been a shepherd boy, was made king of Israel.

GRUMPETTY-GRUMPING JONAH

The Story of Jonah and
the Incredibly Enormous Fish

Grumble

Grumble

Grumble

Jonah wanted to be good. Most of the time, he really did. But, when this big, grown-up man didn't get his own way, he would have the grumpetty-grumps. On and on, he grumbled and grumped. He made such a fuss.

One day God said to Jonah, "I have a job for you."

"That's nice," said Jonah. "What is it?"

"I want you to go to Nineveh," said God. "Tell the people there that they must stop being wicked and start being good, or I shall destroy their city."

"I don't want to go there," grumbled Jonah. "Those people are horrible. They are always fighting and starting wars. They're our enemies. I don't like them."

"But," said God, "I want them to have a chance to be sorry and change."

JONAH, I WANT YOU TO GO TO NINEVEH

"Humpf!" said Jonah. And he went straight to bed.

He didn't sleep. All night he had the grumpetty-grumps. "Don't want to go. It's too far," he grumbled. "And the weather's too hot. Anyway, God's too kind. He won't destroy the city. He won't!"

And then he said, "I know what I'll do…*I'll run away and hide from God!*"

In the morning, Jonah walked to the harbor. He stepped on board a boat and paid his fare. He climbed below deck and he lay down.

"*Huh!* Don't think God will find me here!" he said. And he curled up and fell fast asleep.

The boat sailed off. And where was it going? Not to Nineveh! No, it was going in exactly the opposite direction. To Spain!

After a while, when the boat was far out at sea, there was a storm. Thunder boomed, lightning flashed, and a fierce wind howled. The waves grew higher and higher, wilder and wilder. The boat was tossed up and down, and water came splashing over the side.

The sailors were afraid the boat would sink, so to make it lighter they threw the heavy cargo into the sea.

But still the waves grew higher and higher, wilder and wilder. The sailors prayed to their gods. "Please stop the storm!" they called out. "Please save us from drowning!"

All this time Jonah was below deck, FAST ASLEEP. But one of the sailors remembered him and came down and shook him by the shoulder. "Wake up! The boat is sinking!" the sailor shouted.

When sleepy Jonah came up on deck, all the sailors called out: "Pray to your God, Jonah! Pray! Maybe He will save us!"

"I think…" said Jonah slowly, "I think…this storm is all my fault. I think…you'd better throw me into the sea."

"We can't do that!" said the sailors.

"I think…" said Jonah, "that God is angry with me…because I ran away and tried to hide from Him. So, if you throw me into the sea, the storm will stop, and you will all be safe."

"But you'll drown!" said the sailors.

"If you don't throw me in, we'll *all* drown," said Jonah.

So, feeling very sad, the sailors picked up Jonah and dropped him into the sea.

And the next moment—the storm was over! The sea was calm, a gentle breeze blew, and the boat sailed on.

When Jonah tumbled into the water, he sank down, down, down. He was scared. "Help me, God! Please, help me!" he prayed.

Of course God knew where Jonah was. He was looking after him. And the next moment—an incredibly enormous fish came swimming along. It opened its incredibly enormous mouth and it SWALLOWED JONAH WHOLE.

Glug! glug! glug! Jonah went down its wide fish's throat and landed inside its stomach. It was dark there, and it didn't smell good either. Jonah was very, very scared, and he began to pray.

"Please, God," he said, "please, please get me out of this dark smelly place. I'll do anything you want! I will! I'll go to Nineveh! I promise!"

The fish swam and swam for three days and three nights. And Jonah kept on praying. The fish reached the shore, and *glug! glug! glug!* Jonah shot out of its stomach, up its wide throat, through its incredibly enormous mouth, and landed on a sandy beach. It was not very far from a certain place called…Nineveh!

Jonah was a mess. He had seaweed, fish bones, and goodness knows what else stuck to his clothes and tangled in his hair. But he soon cleaned himself up, washed his clothes, and dried them.

Then God spoke to him again. "Don't forget," He said. "I've got a job for you."

"I know," said Jonah. "I don't want to do it. But I have promised."

"Right then," said God. "Off you go, and tell the wicked people of Nineveh that, *in forty days*, unless they are sorry and start being good, I shall destroy their city."

So off went Jonah, down the road that led to Nineveh.

When he reached the city, he stood in the marketplace shouting: "Forty days! Forty days is all you've got!"

ONLY
4 0
days to
go !!!

Some people laughed at Jonah, but others stopped and listened. Then he told them God's message. Every day he did the same sort of thing, until at last the king heard about Jonah.

"This is serious," said the king. "We are bad people. And I am sorry. I really am. So let's all change and try to be good."

To show he meant what he said, the king took off his fine royal robes and put on rough clothes made from sacks. And instead of sitting on his throne, he sat down on top of a heap of ashes. Then he kept saying, "I am sorry, God, about the bad things I've done. I'll try to be good."

Then *everybody* in Nineveh copied the king. They put on rough clothes made from sacks, sat down on top of a heap of ashes, and kept saying, "Sorry, God, about the bad things. I'll try to be good."

At the end of forty days, God *didn't* send a fire or an earthquake or anything like that to Nineveh. He didn't destroy their city.

The king and his people were very happy. But Jonah was CROSS! He had the grumpetty-grumps. On and on, he grumbled and grumped. He made such a fuss.

"I knew God wouldn't destroy the city," he grumbled. "He's too kind. I knew he would forgive them. I came all this way. And now everyone's going to laugh at me."

Jonah marched outside the city, sat down in the hot sun, and grumbled and grumped some more. The sun beat down on him, hotter and hotter. And Jonah grew crosser and crosser.

God was sorry for Jonah and made a lovely leafy tree spring up beside him. The tree shaded Jonah from the hot sun, and he didn't feel quite so cross. "That's a nice tree," he said.

In the night God made the tree shrivel up and die. The next morning, when the sun beat down, there was no shade. Again Jonah grew hotter and hotter, crosser and crosser.

"I'm sorry you died, tree," said Jonah. "I was fond of you."

Then God spoke to Jonah one more time. "So, Jonah," he said, "you're sorry about the tree!"

"Yes, it was a nice tree," said Jonah. "I'm sorry it died."

"Well," said God, "that's how I felt about the people of Nineveh. I made those people, and I didn't want them to die. So I gave them the chance to be sorry."

"Oh," said Jonah, "I hadn't thought of that."

"And," said God, "I felt the same way about you, Jonah. You didn't do what I asked. You ran away and tried to hide. But I gave you a chance to be sorry and start all over again."

"I'm glad you did," said Jonah.

"In the end, you did what I asked you to do," said God. "And that was good."

So God was pleased with him! This made Jonah feel a whole lot better. The grumpetty-grumps had gone! He jumped up and smiled a big beaming smile.

"Time to go home!" said Jonah. And off he marched!

THE ROARING, SNARLING, HUNGRY LIONS

Brave Daniel's Story

Daniel lived long ago, in the far-off beautiful city of Babylon. He was a clever man, and he was good. Three times every day he knelt by the window of his house and prayed to God.

One day Darius, the mighty king of Babylon, sent for him. "Daniel," he said, "I've heard that you're a clever man, so I want you to be one of my governors. Your job will be to look after some of my lands and people."

"O King," said Daniel, bowing low, "I shall try to be a wise and honest governor."

"I know you will," said King Darius. "I'm sure you won't cheat or steal or tell lies. I trust you."

Now King Darius and most of the people in Babylon were not like Daniel. They did not believe in a living God. They prayed to statues made of gold, clay, stone, or wood. Some even thought King Darius was a god and prayed to him: "O King, live forever! Take care of us! Help us in our troubles!"

King Darius liked that. He was proud, and it made him feel important.

Well, Daniel looked after the king's lands and people wisely and well. He and the king often talked together, and they soon became best friends. And before long, King Darius made Daniel the chief over all his governors.

This made some of the other governors angry and jealous.

"Daniel is too good!" they said. "He never steals or tells lies. And he's too friendly with the king. We'll have to get rid of him!"

But how? They thought and thought. Then what did they do? Those wicked governors went to see King Darius.

They bowed down until their heads touched the floor. "Great King, live forever!" they chanted.

"We are very lucky to have such a great and wonderful king," said one of them.

"We thought," said another, "that because you are so great and wonderful, all the people should pray to you more often. Not just now and then."

"Splendid idea!" said King Darius.

"We thought," said yet another, "you should make a new law. For thirty days, everyone in Babylon must pray only to you. If they pray to a statue or any other god, they must be…THROWN INTO THE LIONS' DEN!"

"Splendid idea!" said King Darius. "Here's the new law. In the next thirty days, if someone prays to any god but me, off they go, *whoof!* STRAIGHT INTO THE LIONS' DEN!"

Those wicked governors smiled. They knew that Daniel believed in one living God and prayed to Him *three times each day.*

Did Daniel hear about the king's new law? Of course he did. But still, next morning, as usual, he knelt by his window and prayed to God. He prayed again at midday, and he prayed in the evening.

And you can guess who stood outside watching Daniel. Those wicked governors. "We've got him now!" they chuckled.

The next morning they hurried off to see King Darius. They bowed till their heads touched the floor and they chanted, "Great King, live forever!"

Then, one wicked governor said, "Daniel has broken your new law. He has prayed to his God."

"*Three times!*" said another. "Right by the window, where anyone can see him."

"Daniel!" exclaimed the king. "Not Daniel! He is my friend!" King Darius was very upset. When he had made the new law, he had forgotten how much Daniel loved his God. Now the king thought and thought. But he couldn't think how to save Daniel.

At last, quietly and sadly, the king said, "I have made a foolish law. But the law must not be broken."

So the king's soldiers were ordered to go and fetch Daniel and throw him into the lions' den.

The lions hadn't been fed that day, and they were very hungry indeed. They prowled around their den, roaring and snarling: *GAROWWW! GRRR-RR-RR!*

As the soldiers marched Daniel down the passage to the den, he could hear the lions' roaring and snarling. He thought, "They sound *very* hungry. But I shall pray to God and try not to be afraid."

When he reached the entrance to the den, he was surprised to see King Darius standing there.

"Daniel, my friend," said the king. "I made a foolish law and I'm sorry. But perhaps your God will keep you safe from the hungry lions."

"I shall pray to my God," said Daniel.

Then the soldiers rolled the huge stone door to one side, and Daniel walked into the lions' den.

Those very hungry lions were still roaring and snarling: GROWWWELL! GRRR-RR-RR! But Daniel just knelt down among them and began to pray.

And those very hungry lions closed their roaring, snarly mouths, lay down, and one by one…
they fell asleep!

When the soldiers rolled the stone door back into place, they listened. And King Darius listened. The lions had stopped roaring and snarling! Had they begun to eat Daniel already? Had they?

King Darius was so upset. He walked slowly back to the palace and went straight to bed. But he couldn't sleep. All night he kept thinking about his friend Daniel and wondering whether Daniel's God could keep him safe from the lions.

As soon as it was light, the king jumped out of bed. He ran through the palace and along the passage leading to the lions' den. He came to the stone door. There was no roaring or snarling. It was very quiet.

"Daniel!" the king shouted. "Did your God hear your prayers and save you from the hungry lions? Answer me, Daniel."

The king put his ear to the door. He listened… and he heard Daniel's voice!

"O King, live forever!" Daniel called. "My God shut the hungry lions' mouths, and, while I prayed, they slept beside me. All night long!"

95

King Darius was so happy. He quickly ordered the
soldiers to open the door. And when Daniel came out
of the den, the king just threw his arms around him.

"Daniel, my friend," said the king, "I'm going to
make a new law. Everyone must now pray to your
God, who kept you safe from the lions. He is the
only God, forever and ever."

Then King Darius made the new law. And he
ordered that the wicked men who wanted to get rid
of Daniel should be...*thrown into the lions' den.*
And they were!

But King Darius and Daniel stayed the best of
friends all their lives.